Your Higher Power is YOU!

Stephen Hartley

Contents

DEDICATION

"This world was never made for one as beautiful as you."[1]

On or about June 6, 2020 I lost my daughter Shannon. We don't know the exact date of her death, as she sadly wasn't found until a few days later. Although her death occurred in the middle of the Covid pandemic, she died because she was an alcoholic.

It was a heartbreak of enormous loss. Still I had to learn to put it behind me, and the writing of this book has been part of my process.

Shannon fought her demons--she had several--but was never able to put them to rest. Underneath all her chaos, she was a sweet and loving child. When she was little I would rock her in my arms and tell her she should never grow up so she could stay as my little girl.

This book is written to help others who feel overwhelmed by life and their personal addictions. At the same time, it is about the existential challenges that we all face.

May everyone find the joy of the most precious jewel--their very Self.

PRAYER OF BLESSINGS

We surround all forms of life with infinite love and compassion. Especially, do we send out compassionate thoughts to those in suffering and sorrow, to those in doubt and ignorance, to all who are striving to attain truth, and to those whose feet stand close to the great change called death. We send forth all wisdom, mercy and love.

May the infinite light of wisdom and compassion so shine within us that the errors and vanities of self may be dispelled. So shall we understand the changing nature of existence and awaken into spiritual peace.

INTRODUCTION

When asked to consider whether we have a higher power, those of us who are settled in religious practice have a ready answer. However, the rest of us tend to be confused by the question. What do we mean by a higher power?

Discussions about God can often end in disagreement because there are so many ways we can conceive of God. Generally the question is whether we *believe* in God on the assumption that we cannot actually *experience* God.

Because people have different concepts of God it is easier if we approach this subject by focusing on our own self--who we really are. The Bible says that God created man in his own image,[2] so we should be able to better understand what we mean by God through examination of our own self.

Buddhism is popular today because in simple terms it follows this approach of avoiding discussions of God, and instead focusing on the cleansing of the heart and mind.

Chapter One

WHERE DO WE START?

All those who are seeking to overcome an addiction, or who are trying to find a sense of inner peace and happiness, must first examine their own mind. To do this, the reader should try a simple meditation practice.

Plan to sit for just ten minutes watching your breath. Watch as you breathe in, pause, and then breathe out. Be the impartial observer of your thoughts, letting them come and go, but recognizing that they are not you the observer.

At the end of the ten minutes take an inventory of your thoughts. What did you think about?

Most of us have repetitive thoughts that are *obsessive and/*or *compulsive.* The thought may be obsessive because it continues over and over again, and it may be compulsive because it repeats even though we would like to be thinking of something else. We find that we have very little control over our thoughts.

Our unhappiness is a sign that our mind is a garbage pail of various negative emotions, such as resentments, jealousy, envy, anger, frustration, guilt, fears, anxiety, loneliness, sorrows, and disappointments.

In addition to what we carry inside of our psyche, simply coping with life itself is a challenge for everyone.

There is a story about a woman, grieving over the loss of her son, who asked the Buddha to bring her son back to life. He promised to help but asked her to first bring a mustard seed from a house that had not been touched by death. So she went from house to house but had no luck as each house had been touched by death in one way or another. With this she realized that everyone had suffered loss.

With unresolved internal psychological issues and problems in the external world coming at us from all directions, it is no surprise that many of us turn to alcohol and drugs or other forms of addiction to dull the pain.

However, there is a better way.

Hidden deep in each of us is a kernel of great beauty and wonder, a source of unending joy, and it is waiting to be discovered and projected outward so that it can be shared with others. Some call this our Higher Power, but *it is really our very own Self*.

I capitalized the "S" in Self to distinguish it from the small self--the ego. The ego is our mental construct of what we perceive ourselves to be, but it really is just a false perception of who we are. Our true Self is there in each one of us, but we are unable to experience it as it is eclipsed by our "garbage pail mind," including the false ego-self.

This book is about how we can free ourselves from everything that holds us back, realize who we truly are and find a happiness that cannot be taken away.

While this book speaks to the reader who is seeking to recover from an addiction, its lessons are the same for anyone seeking to find the precious jewel of inner joy.

Chapter Two

YOUR FIRST STEPS TO A NEW LIFE

The first step in the 12-step program reads as follows:

> *"We admitted we were powerless over alcohol —
> that our lives had become unmanageable."*

There is no step more important than the first step. However, for it to be successful, it must be taken with serious intention and resolve. You must be able to perceive that the path that you are on will never give you the life that you truly want or deserve--a life filled with meaningful relationships, success in your endeavors and inner contentment. Instead, you may have sown chaos and hurt others.

You may be someone who finds it necessary to hide your activities from others because you are not proud of who you are or what you have become. You may have stopped being truthful to yourself or to others.

Those with an alcohol or drug addiction have squandered their sovereignty to their drug of choice, foolishly expecting it to provide the happiness that their soul craves. Sure it provides a temporary payoff, but as time progresses even that payoff slips away.

To put it simply, your life is a mess, and you are miserable. Your ego is in charge and running the ship, but many of its decisions lead to disaster because it is out of control and is not connected to your Higher Power--your true Self.

The Second Step

The second step in the 12-step program reads as follows:

> *"Came to believe that a Power greater than our-selves could restore us to sanity.*

From a spiritual perspective we are much more than our bodies. Think of your body like a car rental. You rent the car for a period of time. At the end of your journey, you turn it in and get a new one. You can also get another one if it gets totaled before your journey is completed. The car is not who you are--it is a vehicle that you inhabit. The body is exactly like that.

You interconnected with EVERYTHING, which we could also call ALL THAT IS. This EVERYTHING and each part of it is imbued with consciousness, a consciousness that is immensely intelligent and knowing. You can call this God, or Allah, or any number of other names and representations of this Supreme Intelligence.

The real YOU, is made of this pure consciousness. Its nature is joyful, and it has not been and can never be tainted by your misconceived actions.

Because this is your real nature, you could say that a promise lives within you. It is the promise that you will in time fully realize and express your potential. When you do, you will find that your life has transformed from chaos to orderliness. Further, you will realize meaning and purpose in your life and become a joy to yourself and others.

Your Real Source of Happiness is Within

Your source of happiness is within. It cannot be found outside of you, in a bottle, a pill or any *thing*. Yes, we experience a thrill when we experience a new relationship, purchase a new car, travel to places we haven't experienced before or accomplish a new goal that we had set for ourselves. However, the initial thrill that accompanies these experiences diminishes over time.

This is because of the impermanent nature of our feelings. We are angry one minute and two hours later we might be able to perceive that our anger was misplaced. The new car in time becomes the old, familiar car. The goal that once excited us is now mundane, and so we need another goal to get excited.

In addition we are poor judges of how much happiness we will derive from realizing new goals or having other new experiences. We mostly discover that things or experiences don't give us the pleasure that we anticipate.[3]

THE THIRD STEP - The Need to Surrender Control

The third step in the 12-step program reads as follows:

"Made a decision to turn our will and our lives over to the care of God as we understood Him."

In the past our tyrant ego has been in control, and it has made a mess of our lives. It thinks only about itself, and therefore does not see or act from the total perspective of ourselves in its relation to other persons and the world at large. It ignores the effect that its actions have on others.

The ego, based on incorrect notions of who we are, tends to act from a platform of its perceived survival rather than from a life of purpose and meaning. When we recognize this, we need to take a decisive step--a step to mark a fundamental change in the direction of our lives. We need to surrender ourselves to our Higher Power.

But what does that mean? It means that we need to open ourselves to that which is most elevated and be willing to allow it to lead on to a new life of discovery and joy that is in accordance with our highest purpose.

Perhaps the Bible verse that best describes this is follows:

> "*Ask, and it will be given to you; search, and you will find; knock, and the door will be opened for you. For everyone who asks receives, and everyone who searches finds, and for everyone who knocks, the door will be opened.*"[4]

To receive we need to ask, and we need to be receptive to the spiritual gifts that we will receive--gifts of greater wisdom and peace, and the awakening of love in our hearts.

What If I Don't Believe in God?

Our belief system doesn't matter. It doesn't matter whether we believe in Jesus, Allah, Krishna or other deities, or whether we are agnostic or atheistic. The internal process of transformation is the same.

As was mentioned in the introduction, Buddhism is non-theistic. Yet, practitioners of Buddhism vigorously work to dispel the false notions of the false ego-self. For some readers, Buddhism may be the "ticket" that you need.

Thich Nhat Hanh, the modern Vietnamese Buddhist Zen master, speaks about our connectedness, not just to our ancestors, friends, and relatives, but to EVERYTHING. He coined the term "interbeing" to describe this truth. He wrote:

"Everything relies on everything else in the cosmos
in order to manifest—whether a star, a cloud, a
flower, a tree, or you and me."[5]

Realization of this truth leads us to be a more caring and compassionate person. Love itself is the expression of this truth of our existence.

If you practice the suggestions in this book, as time goes by you will start to think of yourself in different terms--not as a small isolated entity, but as part of the whole, i.e. the broader Self. Then your life will take on tremendous purpose and meaning.

The process of Self-discovery always contains the following key elements:

1 - We recognize that we are "off the track" and that our life is not working.

2 - We consciously connect to our "Higher Power" or "Higher Self" to lead us in a new direction.

3 - We start to make significant changes in our life to actualize our new purpose.

The elements of transformation apply to everyone, even to those who are not burdened by an alcohol, drug, or other addiction.

THE FOURTH STEP

The fourth step in the 12-step program reads as follows:

"Made a searching and fearless moral inventory of ourselves."

Dealing With Guilt and Shame

When leading an ego-driven life we always leave behind a trail of parties that we have injured along the way, whether physically or emotionally. It is good to focus on our failings, because they help us to stick with our resolve to lead a better life. It helps to make the effort to contemplate how our actions have impacted others. However, it is important not to allow ourselves to wallow in guilt and shame.

Those who embark on a journey to a transformative life are often burdened by thoughts and feelings that, due to their past, they will never be able to give up their addictions or make the changes necessary to be a different person.

However, such thoughts should be eschewed as they can be an obstacle. Everyone seeking to change their life must battle such negative thoughts. Life is for learning, and we can and do learn from our mistakes.

Your real Self is itself Divine in nature, and nothing can touch its purity. You are like a clean mirror that is covered with some dust. Just blow off the dust and your mirror will again be able to reflect the light of the Sun.

This truth is reflected in the Parable of the Prodigal Son.[6] In this story a son asks his father for his inheritance, but then squanders it in profligate living. He comes upon misfortune and returns home repentant, asking his father only to work for wages. The father is so jubilant he throws a party to celebrate the son's return, over the objection of his other son who had been good all along.

Have Confidence that You will Succeed!

The important thing is to make the resolve to change your life. If you do, you will not be held back from realizing your potential.

Your first step, if taken with the totality of your intention and deliberation, must eventually lead to the goal, just as the solitary stream high in the mountains eventually joins and becomes lost in a raging river, the force of which inevitably finds its way to the ocean. The downward flow only goes in one direction. All our efforts to make ourselves a better person lead back to our very Source.

Chapter Three

THERE ARE MANY WAYS TO APPROACH THE DIVINE

No religion or spiritual practice has exclusive rights to the Divine. You are free to choose the path that feels right for you, and for most of us it changes along the way.

Likewise, for those inclined to worship, there is no deity or form that singularly represents God or Source. The Divine will manifest for us in the form that best meets our expectations. For those of us who are not inclined to worship the Divine in the form of a deity, it will manifest as light, what Buddhists call "the Clear Light of the Void," or possibly as an enveloping and comforting darkness, empty of all sensations.

The Real Meaning of the 2nd Commandment

Worshiping the Divine in the form of a deity with form is considered by many to be prohibited by the Second Commandment of the Hebrew Bible, which reads:

> *"You shall not make for yourself an idol, whether in the form of anything that is in heaven above or that is on the earth beneath or that is in the water under the earth. You shall not bow down to them or serve them..."[7]*

It is all a matter of attitude and intention. In worshiping the Divine in the form of a deity or other form it is important to realize that you are worshiping specific qualities of the Divine represented by that deity. The Divine itself is beyond human comprehension, but manifests in various forms, just as a prism separates light into its various colors. Each deity is like a specific portal to the Divine.

Just as you remember that the rainbow is created from clear light as you focus on a specific color, you must remember that you are worshiping a quality of the Divine as you direct your loving attention to a deity.

The other important aspect of any form of worship is that the worship should be for the purpose of approaching the Divine, and not for the purpose of attaining worldly goals. Your purpose should be to establish a loving relationship with the Divine.

The Divine Feminine

In this age we are examining the ways in which men have dominated our culture. However, to be complete we need to be a harmonious blend between the masculine and the feminine--between thought and emotion, between knowledge and love.

Likewise, we will never be able to approach the Divine if we lead with our "rational" brain, because the knowledge of truth can only be experienced with the open heart, as it is beyond the thinking mind.

Religion is always in part a function of culture, and so religion also has been affected by our male-dominant culture. This is very apparent in the Catholic Church, which still does not permit females to assume the role of a priest. Still, in the Catholic Church we have seen the elevation of Mary as a dominant figure, and the recitation of the rosary as a recommended practice.

In the Hindu religion, various female deities, such as Kali, Durga and Sita have prominent roles and have become objects of worship. Moreover, the worship of the Divine feminine is considered necessary to bring the Divine down to the energetic level.

For all these reasons it is important to remember that the Divine can be approached in many ways.

Chapter Four

HEALING OUR BROKENNESS

Underneath every addiction is suffering. In our emotional body all of us have some elements of hurt and brokenness that we carry around with us everywhere we go. In using the term "addiction" in this context we mean not just drug or alcohol use, but also unhealthy clinging to others or experiences that may not be healthy for us.

Naturally we prefer not to think about our internal sore spots and are drawn to anything that will allow us to dull the pain. There are many ways we can accomplish this. Almost all of us rely heavily on every manner of distractions, such as sports games, internet surfing, social media, TV and movie dramas, comedies, and competitions.

Many of us are afraid to spend time by ourselves as when the distractions fade we may come face to face with our hurts and fears. Still, it is best to recognize these sore spots in ourselves and take the necessary steps to provide healing. It is also important to remember that we have or will experience suffering in our life, although the causes of the suffering may differ. In your suffering you are not alone.

Observe and Heal Your Brokenness

Instead of distracting our way out of the pain, it is best to direct our attention to the places in our heart that require healing. For some, this will mean spending time with a psychotherapist who can help us find a way to frame the hurt in a way that will give us a different perspective. Talking with friends may help to accomplish this task.

Others may find it useful to meditate on the moments that caused us pain, the wounds from that experience, our reactions that may have been harmful to another, and embrace it all in a loving embrace.

It is useful to remember and acknowledge that all difficult experiences are tools for learning and can facilitate our growth. Our constant practice should be to replace negative thoughts, whether about ourselves or others, with positive and loving thoughts. As we continue with this practice we will grow in greater happiness and fulfillment.

Forgiveness

When others have caused harm to us we are often saddled with resentment, which causes our emotional wounds to fester. Until we are willing to surrender that resentment and embrace forgiveness, our emotional wound will be incapable of healing. When we hold on to many resentments towards others, we are weakened and prevented from ever realizing our potential.

Avoiding Judgment

In our daily practice we should remember to avoid judging others, as such thoughts have the effect of preventing us from moving forward. We must remember that we cannot ever fully understand the reasons for another's behavior. Often the person causing the harm has himself been subject to ill treatment and so far has been unable to process their hurt.

Gratitude

When we focus on the harm that others have caused in our life, or the circumstances that have thwarted our desires, it only has the effect of bringing our spirits down. On the other hand, focusing on the many things that are positive in our life, many of which we take for granted, has the opposite effect.

If our eyes are open to it, we truly live in a world of tremendous magic, with the variety of flowers and other flora in abundance, the variety of birds and other animals with whom we share this planet. If on a daily basis everyone on our planet considered what they were grateful for, would we be creating all of the wars and disharmony that plague this planet?

Suffering is Ennobling

Know that all suffering is ennobling and most suffering is temporary. Feelings come and go. If you work actively to embrace your suffering and the losses that you have endured, you WILL learn and grow from the experience.

Take the High Road

When others have caused us harm, we do not need to retaliate. Sure, there are times when we do not want to communicate passivity, weakness, or vulnerability. However, when our safety is not threatened, we need not return hatred or harm, as doing so simply reinforces a negative loop of emotions and actions.

Chapter Five

PULLING UP THE ROOTS OF OUR SUFFERING

"All I can hear
I me mine, I me mine, I me mine
Even those tears
I me mine, I me mine, I me mine"[1]

When we start our journey inward, we can see that most of our thoughts are centered around ourselves. However, this preoccupation with our self (thoughts such as enriching or protecting ourselves, blaming others for our troubles, etc.) only creates more suffering.

Buddhism identifies five primary roots of suffering. All these are binding--i.e. not liberating. These are:

Ignorance of our true nature - We do not know who we truly are. We identify ourselves with our physical body and think we are nothing more. However, the truth is that we are eternal, divine beings who are not affected by the suffering of our physical body. When we see ourselves in this light, we are able to create a sense of distance between ourselves and the troubles of our physical bodies. The same applies to suffering that we experience on an emotional level.

The fear of death - This fear, which generally lurks in the background of our mind, tends to dominate our thinking. Many of our actions are dominated by the thought of wanting to do or experience things before we die. Time feels compressed and we become anxious.

Egoism - When our ego dominates our thinking we become a slave to fulfill its demands because it is never content. Remember that it is only a construct of our minds. Hidden within it is a little child that feels that it is "less than..." and needs to prove it is better than others.

Attachment to pleasure - If we find an experience to be pleasurable, we are driven to repeat the pleasure, although often we find successive experiences to be less pleasurable than the first. We may engage in actions that are harmful to others or to ourselves so that we can repeat pleasurable experiences. In addition, we may experience frustration and disappointment and/or anger directed to others if our efforts are thwarted.

Aversion and fear - Unpleasurable experiences cause us to engage in behaviors to avoid their recurrence and we develop fear of the experience. The fear itself weakens us and creates anxiety.

Chapter Six

THE JOY OF MINDFULNESS

"After recognizing 'I am that from whom the universe springs like waves from the sea,' why run around so pitifully?"[1]

When we look around, we see people at leisure are busy with all types of activities--talking on the telephone, perusing social media, taking pictures or videos, watching movies, traveling to enjoy new experiences, attending social gatherings, etc.

The activities engaging our attention are endless. However, while these activities may provide enjoyment, they all draw our attention outward. Are we afraid to be alone with our thoughts?

It is important that we build into our day some time for meditation or inward reflection. As we do, we come face to face with all the thought patterns that are holding us hostage. If we just stay with those thoughts as an observer, as desperate or unhappy as they may be, in time a beautiful change takes place. We start to experience the inner joy that is hidden inside of us--our very nature.

The practice of mindfulness can continue throughout the day.

Turn off the radio in your mind and observe what is around you. Watch the wind cause the trees to dance. See the patterns of the clouds. Watch the people around you tend to their activities. Most of the time we are so distracted by our inner dialogue we do not notice the world around us.

See the Divine at play in a tree, in the birds, the movement of the air as it shakes the leaves, the ripples in the water, a caterpillar as it tries to climb up a twig or an old lady sitting on a park bench. It can be seen in the face of an ordinary man, in a sunset or an array of clouds, in the peace of a meadow or lake, the love of a friend, in the silence of our Being. The Divine is never completely hidden if you truly have eyes to see.

Know that not only your life, but each moment is full of purpose. Do every simple task as though it is the only important task in the entire world. Feel that nothing else requires your attention. Learning to flow with and center in each moment as it comes. Step into the river of that moment and let the current take you and flow through you. Be open to how you can be a channel of the Divine.

Know that it is possible to be calm inwardly while living an active life, just as a wheel's center of rotation is motionless while every other point on the wheel is in motion.

Remember the mortality of your physical body and live each moment with intense purpose as if it were your last day. What would truly matter to you if this were your last day?

Remember that all that you truly need is in you! Honor yourself. Give up all ideas of weakness and being less than.

You can leave behind all the desperation of being in dire need of things and experiences.

Further, give up your dependency and don't give your power to anyone or anything!

When you observe a city from a tall building you observe both other buildings, immobile, and the vehicles on the city streets that are in constant motion. The real you is like the immovable landscape of buildings, and everything else about you--your body, thoughts and emotions, are like the vehicles in constant motion. **That which is immovable is the real you.** The Divine and *your very Self* are the ground of all being.

These statements may seem crazy to most readers, but they are the absolute truth. Resolve that you will remember this despite all your troubles and seek to reach that level of understanding in which you will KNOW these statements to be true.[10]

Chapter Seven

CHANGING FROM ME TO WE

"Only love is real
Everything else illusion"[1]
Carol King

Most of our sense of duality comes from the perception of scarcity. However, while in the world of economics there may be a scarcity of goods, on the spiritual level scarcity does not exist at all. It is only an illusion of the unreal world in which we live.

Practice seeing the Divine everywhere, and each moment as being miraculous. Penetrate each moment of disharmony with your wisdom and love.

Concentrate on expressing joy and happiness to those with whom you come in contact. Try to find something to give to each person. Know that in giving you are the person receiving as well as the person giving.

See each person as an expression of the Divine and learn to love unconditionally, especially the broken as they need our love, not our judgment. Know that your thoughts are extremely powerful and constantly project love.

If you continue with this practice you will start seeing the world in a new light, and finally discover who you truly are.

Remember that your spiritual journey is your own. Let no one tell you the "right way." As long as you are sincere and are opening yourself to greater love and compassion for others and all life, then you are on the right path.

The discovery of your own Self can be compared to waking up on a crisp, cool morning, after a vigorous storm that raged the night before. All the chaos and struggle has been washed away, now leaving only a cloudless sky. The sun is rising in its full glory, illuminating everything that had until then been hidden by the darkness. There is joy in the heart, because the storm is over, not to return.

1. Lyrics taken from the Don McLean song entitled "Vincent"

2. Genesis 1:27

3. Psychologists have verified the truth of this statement. See Stumbling Upon Happiness by Daniel Gilbert. Vintage (2007)

4. Matthew 7:7-8. New Revised Standard Version Updated Edition

5. From The Art of Living by Thich Nhat Hanh. Harper-Collins 2017.

6. Luke 15:11-32

7. Exodus 20: 4-5

8. Lyrics taken from the Beatles song "I Me Mine."

9. Ashtavakra Gita, Verse 3.3 Translation by Janki Parikh

10. The author's book Pure One explores these ideas in more detail.

11. Lyrics from "Only Love is Real," a song by Carol King

Printed in Great Britain
by Amazon

Stowaways

ANDRÉ ACIMAN

Stowaways

faber

First published in 2026
by Faber & Faber Ltd
The Bindery, 51 Hatton Garden
London ECIN 8HN

Typeset by Faber & Faber Ltd
Printed in the UK by CPI Group (UK) Ltd, Croydon, CRO 4YY

This is a work of fiction. All of the characters, organisations and events
portrayed in this novel are either products of the author's imagination
or are used fictitiously

A CIP record for this book
is available from the British Library

ISBN 978-0-571-39992-5

MIX
Paper | Supporting
responsible forestry
FSC® C013604

Printed and bound in the UK on FSC® certified paper in line with our continuing
commitment to ethical business practices, sustainability and the environment.
For further information see faber.co.uk/environmental-policy

Our authorised representative in the EU for product safety is
Easy Access System Europe, Mustamäe tee 50, 10621 Tallinn, Estonia
gpsr.requests@easproject.com

2 4 6 8 10 9 7 5 3 1

For Alex

Para siempre

Carol's email arrived late on a hot July evening while Julian was watching a crime series with Dennis, his husband. The two had just finished dinner and were sitting on the sofa with the air conditioner whirring at full blast. A typical midweek summer evening in Manhattan, when nothing, not cold showers, not cold drinks, not a desultory, long stroll through the chilly aisles of an all-night drugstore, could undo the heat's hold on the city. July weather. The will sags, sloth sets in, the mind nods and nothing gets done.

That's how Julian felt when he saw the email flash on his phone that evening. He didn't want to give it a thought. He had never met or heard of her, and out of sheer indifference after a morning spent arguing in court, he would have immediately deleted it had it not been for its subject line: *From Paul Axel.* An email from a dead man? he wondered. Then, realizing that it came from a third party, he decided to keep it, figuring it would announce either a memorial service for Paul or some charity sponsored by the man's family.

Following the end of the evening's episode they'd been streaming, he remembered to look at the email while Dennis was stowing dishes in the dishwasher. Her email was very short and informed him that she had a message from Paul Axel but would prefer to relay it in person. She was leaving with her husband for a two-week vacation in Sicily, so *she would appreciate* if he'd manage to find a brief moment to meet her *kind of soonish. Kind of soonish,* which she'd italicized, preceded by the snub-nosed *appreciate,* not italicized, was clearly her way of saying ASAP. Raspy, bossy, a touch too curt and, ultimately, presumptive. But never mind, he thought. He seldom emailed anyone past ten at night.

At six the next morning, before even reading the online headlines of the *Guardian* and the *FT*, he replied with a gracious *Of course.* She immediately shot back with two words: *When, where?*

He waited a while before replying, then suggested Friday at ten in the morning outside the Bryant Park Grill. If it got too hot, perhaps they could sit and have coffee at the Grill itself. *Let's meet inside the Grill. Much quieter,* she replied. He agreed. Friday, he explained, was usually a light day for him. He couldn't remember if the Grill was open at ten, but the plan she proposed was to meet by the Grill and then decide.

Lawyers at his firm dressed down on Fridays; some didn't even come to the office. He was a litigator, he explained, and had a difficult case the next week and needed to gather some papers at the office, make a few phone calls and then rush to Penn Station to head to the beach for the long weekend. *When are you coming back?* she asked, totally ignoring his chatty details about work or his race to the house on the beach. *Tuesday*, he replied. By then, she'd have left for Sicily, she wrote. *Grill works*, was her message back. It was so very to the point that it almost felt like a harmless pinprick that left you wondering why it hurt. *P.S.*, she wrote back, *your name came up many times in his journals, but more when I see you.* Julian had no idea what all this was about.

Carol was curious to meet Julian. She had drawn what she thought was a fairly good picture of him from Paul's journals that she and Anna Livia, Paul's daughter, had recently deposited at the New York Public Library. Months earlier, she had asked Anna Livia for permission to read the journals. Permission was granted right way, since Anna Livia had known her from her earliest childhood and was fully aware of her friendship with her father. They had had the handwritten pages scanned ever so neatly onto a flash drive; the rest, from the mid-eighties on, he'd written using his various computers. They had three copies made of both the handwritten journals and those on computer and transferred them onto three flash drives: one for Anna Livia and another for Carol. They'd offered to make a copy for Connie, Paul's wife, but she wanted nothing to do with it. Connie had loved him from the very start, loved him enough to turn thoroughly hostile when she saw he'd grown indifferent to her.

As Carol and Anna Livia headed to the library to hand over both the physical hard copies and the drive, Anna Livia said that these would be made available with her written permission. It surprised her to know that people might want to read them, but Paul did have lots of friends and many might want to leaf through his pages.

'What will you do with your copy?' Anna Livia had asked. 'Read them occasionally,' Carol replied. But she knew that she wanted to read and reread what Paul had written about her during their first years in college when she'd asked him point-blank to kiss her as she rested against a cold, ugly wall. A year later they met at a party on Charles Street, made love, broke up, and never slept together again. But the best was when they'd go together to their college library every night, first to translate *Animal Farm* into ancient Greek and then to read Dante together. At first, they'd go to a bar close to the library, until going to the bar became an established ritual that both liked to pretend wasn't quite set down and was somehow always improvised at the last minute, which is why they laughed whenever either feigned to forget about the bar before heading back to their respective dorms. They read each other's minds. They liked thinking alike. That was so very long ago, she thought. Anna Livia was almost thirty now. It struck Carol as ironic that Anna Livia was now ten years older than Carol had been in their college years.

An entire life in one tiny flash drive, the daughter had said while she and Carol were leaving the library after meeting the curator.

'I didn't understand who my father was until I read his pages,' she said. 'I know him better now but I loved him more before.'

Maybe we love people because they won't let us know them, Carol had wanted to say but kept quiet. It was the kind of thing Paul would have said. After knowing him all these years, and especially after reading his journals, you couldn't help but mine the man's love for paradox and what could never be proven.

Sometimes the things he said hovered like a tentative compromise between unkempt wisdom and polished nonsense. He loved these hypothetical insights built on air: *We love those we cannot know. It's our first and last move. Intimacy*, he used to say, *is best with strangers. We're seldom who we are with those we know.*

During the months she read Paul's journal, Carol spent more time in his head than she'd done throughout their long relationship. With his thoughts totally open to her, she had lived with him, understood him better and grown to love the man despite his cunning, snarky quips about her behaviour that left her feeling angry and exposed. She never thought that someone as heedless as Paul could cut through what she believed were her inviolate shields. How easily he'd unmasked her jittery, sham excuses for always arriving late when it was clear they couldn't wait to be together. And how feckless her diversions had been whenever he started to recall their night together after they'd met at the party on Charles Street following their graduation. When he did try to share his memory of that night, she'd reminded him that it might as well never have happened. But these moments surfaced in his journal count-less times, both while they were occurring and as he kept remembering them years later, as if nosing for bones he'd inadvertently bur-ied there and was trying to recover with the unyielding hope of an ageing detective still searching for a DNA match long after his sus-pect had been imprisoned, found guilty and executed. She preferred to let on she couldn't recall the when or where of whatever they'd said and done. All of it belonged to what she'd once called *erstwhile and elsewhere stuff*. Except when she had a touch to drink or needed to pretend she'd had more to drink than she was used to. She'd be with her husband and he with Connie and because it felt safer in their company, that look would pass between them, then he knew, because she wanted him to know, that their *erstwhile and elsewhere* hadn't petered away but, like an item on consignment, was easy to revisit, never redeemed. It was, in the words he'd often used in his journal, in permanent abeyance – i.e., not happening, never to happen. In his pages, though, their first kiss had permanently altered his life or, as he wrote, *ground his life to a halt.* The rest of life was just treading water. *At twenty-two on that November night, I stopped growing*, he'd written. *The years piled on, but time had stopped.*

Just let it go! she had once said to him. She was right. He'd even transcribed those very words. *Just let it go!* But he couldn't let it go. What she'd really meant was *I haven't forgotten a thing, don't you ever forget either, but never bring it up.* Silence and a mere glance was how they brought it up when they couldn't help themselves. Silence was good enough, silence said everything, silence had come before life and would endure long after they put the lid over their bodies. *We never asked for life, we didn't ask to be born. Whoever needed love when the price was so high?* he'd once said.

Now, after spending so much time with his pages, she could claim to know him better than anyone else. If he were alive today, she'd want him dead, never forgive him, and swear never to have a thing to do with him. He had loved her without rest or remission, he once wrote, as if his love were a sin impossible to expiate. He struggled with it, denied it, mocked it and was worn down by it till simple boredom took over and redefined all he touched, finally drowning him in his own bathtub on a weekend afternoon when his wife was out.

She recognized him right away from the four pictures that Paul had copied from the web and inserted into his journal. In each photo, Julian is wearing his default bow tie. He came wearing one now. Still, she hadn't expected someone in his late thirties. He too seemed to have spotted her on arriving at their designated spot. 'Closed until 11:30' read the sign at the Bryant Park Grill. 'Pity,' he said, indicating the sign. It was, as they had both anticipated, a very hot and muggy morning. 'May get worse,' he added, making a passing comment about the weather, seeing she was silent. 'We'll sit outside then,' she said. He needed a cup of coffee from across the street. She'd wait for him, she said. 'Just don't take too long,' she added, still finding something vaguely unseemly in his claim to *need* a cup of coffee. But then she said she'd like coffee too and would walk with him. She paid for the two of them. Together they headed back to one of the tiny round metal tables painted orange and scattered outside the Grill.

'Was that the Starbucks where you used to meet Paul every morning?'

'Yes.'

When they sat down, 'So who starts?' she asked. He looked up at her with a puzzled look. What did she mean? She didn't give him time to wonder, nor did she answer his slightly befuddled glance. 'Then I'll start,' she said.

'Yes, maybe you should, as I have no idea about any of this.'

'*This*,' she hissed, echoing the word, as though scoffing at it with marked censure. But then she let it go. She emptied two packets of sugar into her coffee and, with the stirrers she had picked up at the counter, mixed the sugar in with determined, skittish motions of the hand that signalled her irascible temperament. She put the lid on her cup, took one hasty sip, took another to give the coffee a second chance, then made up her mind and placed the cup down as far from her as she could.

'Let me just start by saying that Paul was in love with me. He'd been in love with me for decades. When we met, I was barely eighteen, he was twenty.'

This seemed to lead to the question he was clearly meant to ask.

'Were you also in love with him?' he asked, more out of courtesy than because he was interested.

'Difficult to say. I'd like to say no, but in his journal, he always believed I was denying it. Maybe he was right. I did love him, but more like a brother, though he definitely had no brotherly feelings for me. We got very close to becoming regular lovers once – we spent a night together, but then I held back because something stood in his way as well. What that something was in either of us is anyone's guess.

'I did, by mistake, bring up our night together many years later, but either he had changed his mind and didn't want to discuss it, or pretended

not to understand, or simply failed to pick up
my cue. Come to think of it, mine was a very
veiled cue, and I can see why he'd deny there
was anything like a hint in my words. He too
tried to bring up that night. My turn to sweep
it under the rug. A mound of denials and defer-
rals stood between us. You could never tell if
what bound us was stronger than what kept us
apart. Both were powerful drives, to the point
that over the years we saw clearly enough that
when I was drawn to him, he'd turn his back,
and when he was drawn to me, I was out the
door. We knew that we'd always remain excep-
tionally close – closer by far than either of our
spouses would have wanted, though the two of
us were champions at disguising it both from
them and from ourselves. So, the short answer
to your question: did I love him? Yes. Did he
love me? Yes. But it all depends on how you
define the word love, which no one, as far as I
know, has ever been able to do.'

'Do you miss him?' His questions were naive and predictable, and they made her want to smile. But then he had nothing to go on, poor fellow, and was clearly groping his way. She imagined him as a young public defender carrying a yellow legal pad taking notes with a ballpoint pen that he kept nervously clicking on and off each time the detainee went over the details of his alibis.

She repeated his question. 'Do I miss him?' That question was too personal and had come too soon, she thought. But then he was asking what she'd obviously set him up to ask. She wanted time to think and to answer with a degree of blunt candour that she prided herself on. But the answer had never really crossed her mind.

'I don't really miss him. But this may not make sense to you. I don't miss him because he isn't really dead for me, or is only dead for a while, as though he had gone to buy cigarettes and hadn't come back yet. Death doesn't last forever, you know. Sometimes we spent years apart, not talking, not even writing. So separations were more the rule than the exception. One night, eons ago, he did tell me how much he loved me. I think he'd never said this to anyone without lying. I told him I loved him too and would always love him. That was decades ago when we ran into each other at a party on Charles Street. We made love that night. But ours was happenstance love. It couldn't last. Yet I know that he was always thinking of me, as I was thinking of him. There was no ache on either of our parts, or maybe only an occasional, superficial paper cut. Nothing ever really crippled him or me. Paper cuts were easy to ignore.'

'Easy to deny?'

'Easy to deny,' she agreed.

It irked her that she had acquiesced so readily to his passing correction. 'Maybe ours was

17

not denial, but abstention,' she immediately corrected so as not to yield so quickly to the young lawyer.

'But abstention is no better than denial, don't you think?' he asked.

He's young but not stupid, she thought, and he could just be right.

'Yes, it's no better,' she finally conceded. She liked people who had an edge. Paul had that edge. She had it too. In most cases their edge was a curious blend of insight and irony but with something redemptive thrown in so as not to leave their indictment of mankind so binding. The lawyer might share her way of thinking, she thought, but she wasn't sure yet.

Julian gave an imperceptible nod to her answer, uncertain whether to trust her hasty agreement or read in her initial correction a reluctance to concede to someone else's insight. He was trying to decipher why this intimidating woman sitting beside him had wanted to meet him. He noticed she was just staring at her coffee long after he'd drunk his. Maybe she simply wanted to talk about Paul for a while and thought he might have information to disclose. But he had nothing to share and kept absent-mindedly wrapping his soft plastic coffee stirrer around one of his fingers. It made the stirrer look like a Cracker Jack ring, she thought, observing his gesture as another proof that, despite his sharp mind, Julian was still a kid. Paul had written about Julian's weekends in the Hamptons playing volleyball, then drinking, the quick swim first thing in the morning, the dinners al fresco with housemates and friends, none of whom knew how to cook and couldn't care less that none could – all of it so hauntingly present in Paul's journals after he'd culled scattered details about the Hamptons from conversations with Julian. A boy, she thought, even his smile was boyish.

She didn't have time to continue thinking of the beach scenario because the young lawyer finally spoke. 'Pardon my asking, Carol, but why am I here?' She recalled Paul's take on Julian: very matter-of-fact, dry, dull, methodical, solid, sometimes blank, but then maybe intentionally blank – a born litigator, Paul had written. 'Where do I fit in all this?' Julian asked again.

'*This?*' She repeated the word with that same emphatic derision bordering on scorn which she'd used just a few moments earlier. She could almost hear the impatient clock of the lawyer's billing hours clicking in the background. 'We'll get to that,' she said. 'Did you know Paul well?'

'I knew him, but not well. He invited my husband and me a couple of times to celebrations and cocktails at the magazine. Sometimes I thought he invited us to fill the room with people.'

'Paul had no need to fill a room. He had adoring friends all over the city,' she snapped, then paused a moment. 'So, you really don't know why he'd invite you to his office party every year?'

'No. He was the editor of a prestigious journal, and I was flattered that he'd think of me as an acquaintance. We'd frequently bump into each other at the Starbucks across the street, and we'd exchange a few humorous words each time. I still remember running into each other buying a muffin on Yom Kippur after we'd found out that we were both Jewish. It made the two of us laugh. He was usually very forthcoming, very cheerful, while I, quite honestly, was reluctant to impose, so I kept my distance a bit.'

'But you did attend his events.'

'Of course.'

'And you still have no idea.'

'No idea about what?'

This man was either being completely stupid

or intentionally naive. How could he not have known, guessed, or even figured out, or had he decided to ignore it? *Five years, for God's sake, you've been in his journal for five years and you had no idea?*

His blank look unnerved her. By now at least he might have guessed. But the boy wasn't guessing.

'Can't you see?'

'What can't I see?'

'Paul was in love.'

'With you, yes.'

'No, dear,' she stopped a moment, 'in love with you.'

He looked totally baffled.

'Me?'

'Totally and hopelessly in love. He's been in love with you for five years. You're all over his journal. I wouldn't have known otherwise.'

'But he was married and had a daughter and had a life and all.'

'And so?' she asked, raising one shoulder, suggesting annoyance and disbelief.

Julian was dumbstruck.

She recalled the exact entry in his journal, she said. Julian had just purchased his morning coffee at Starbucks and, while picking it up and holding his leather briefcase in the same hand, had accidentally spilled his entire cup on the counter. Paul immediately grabbed a few napkins and rushed to help him dab the coffee and, after the two managed to clean the counter as best they could, Julian gave Paul so bountiful a sunlit, flushed smile that he fell for it without caution or hindrance, because so radiant a thank-you smile held the promise of something he was willing to stake years of his life to see again. That night he didn't sleep a wink and by dawn the memory of Julian's smile had swollen into full-fledged longing, and finally, finally into love, because love was the last and costliest admission of all, the cut that never heals, the one you put off naming because you know there's no coming back.

The morning after the coffee spill, Paul was at Starbucks. He was old enough to know he shouldn't be there and he couldn't help but laugh at himself. *I'll look ridiculous*, he thought. *I know*, his journal replied. But he was there.

'When he saw you at Starbucks, the joke was irresistible. "Spilled any coffee this morning?" You smiled and said no. He tried the same question the following morning but by then the joke had dimmed, and you were back to simple nods, sometimes even silence. He noticed once that you kept staring at him while he had started talking to you, and that set his heart racing, though he was insecure enough to think you hadn't recognized him and that this was how you looked at a stranger who'd started speaking to you out of nowhere. You'd clearly forgotten about the spilled coffee. It's in his journal.

'Meanwhile, he had figured out at what time you were likely to stop at Starbucks in the morning and made a point of bumping into you there, not too frequently at first, because he didn't want you to know. But then he did want you to know – or, as always with our dear Paul, he wavered between hoping you'd know and dreading you might. He feared heading to Starbucks every morning, not because he had grown to care for you and was addicted to a perfunctory morning nod, but because rearranging his whole day for a fifteen-second greeting threw him down a degrading spiral from which he needed the whole day to re-cover. Once, when he was far later for his coffee and was resigned not to see you that morning, there you were, taking your time at a table – you seldom sat at a table – and he was almost tempted to hope you had waited on purpose to run into him. But no, he thought again, it was an accident. That too is in his journal.

'Nothing ever came of it. He scanned his life, the years before and those after, and they looked so hollow, so wasted. *Just love away*, he told himself, *and smuggle the whole thing under your pillow, your blanket, your lonely life.*'

Contraband love, he called it, speaking with Carol once, the shame and the pity of it.

'By then we had become friends again and, though I believed that a part of him still pined for me, he frequently alluded to all kinds of romances. But then – and here is an interesting fact—'

'Tell me.'

The boy is biting, she thought, and she relished it.

'He told me he'd met someone. He even told me that he'd meet that person at Starbucks almost every morning. "Does Connie know?" I asked, being her friend as well. "No, she don't know nothing," he replied, trying to inject humour into his admission. "How come?" I asked. "I do nothing with that other person and am still the same man with Connie," he explained. Then I couldn't resist: "Are you the same man with me?" "I am with you, have always been, but I like that other person too." "That other person has no pronoun?" I finally asked. "That other person won't have one for the time being," he replied, at which we both laughed, since we understood what the pronoun was.'

'I assume I'm the one without the pronoun,' said Julian.

'Yes, you're the one without the pronoun. Paul was not a stalker, but he was eventually able to cull quite a bit about you. Having guessed you were a creature of habit, it was not difficult for him to figure out that you'd show up at Starbucks for coffee every morning. He wanted to know everything about you, most likely because he was hoping to find a chink in the armour, a tiny fissure that might allow him to hope – hope for what, though? Maybe to make a move? Not Paul, though. He once told you that the two of you should have breakfast in a better place one day. By then you were speaking briefly every time you met before heading to your respective offices. You even greeted him first sometimes, which surprised him and did indeed rouse his attention, since he'd always felt that if he didn't say hello, you'd never have done so yourself. You responded enthusiastically to the invitation for breakfast but he didn't trust it, didn't think you really meant it. So he never followed up on the invitation. You never did either, which confirmed his suspicion. You were ducking the invitation, and he was feigning to forget. It occurs to me now that the place for a late breakfast could easily have been the Grill here. Don't you think?'

'I vaguely remember his mentioning breakfast once. But I was sure he'd changed his mind or just forgotten.'

'No, it hurt him.'

'We were both regular coffee addicts –
breakfast would have been so easy and I would
have loved it.'

Turning to her, he noticed she had not
drunk her coffee. Why had she even bought it?

'All this gives me no pleasure. But I am so
glad we met,' she said, with a tone of closure
in her voice.

He agreed with her.

'But tell me one last thing,' he asked, 'how
did you find me?'

She was about to answer but the answer was
so obvious: 'Let me guess, in his journal!'

It made them both laugh.

'No, not in his journal. He had sent me an
email asking me to meet you if something
should happen to him. Who would have
thought?' She stopped a moment. 'He told his
daughter to read his journal but only when he
was gone, and not to be too shocked by what

she'd find there. To which she said, "I'm old enough, Dad, I can handle it." Then he added in passing and not without a chuckle – which is how he always expressed what mattered most – that he'd had two lifelong heartbreaks. "Dad, I said I could handle it, okay?" She didn't want to discuss his love life. "But there are some people who might want to know how I felt. Let them read my journal." He jotted down my most recent email for her and then sent me yours a week before dying. As he was writing down your name, I'm sure he was already savouring an extended dose of happiness that ordinary life couldn't grant him. The thought that we would find out about his love was like his surrogate avowal. His silence may have compelled him to take his own life, but leave it to Paul to find a way around death.'

She paused and thought a while.

'To me his journal is goodbye love. As for

you, Julian, you might tell your friends, you might even laugh about it over dinner in the Hamptons, but I know that our moment together here has made him smile.'

Julian was listening, trying to rein in the scatter of thoughts in his mind.

'To me,' he said, 'this confession sounds like a last-ditch message in a bottle. Maybe you can't reply to a message in a bottle, but you feel reckless if you destroy either the bottle or the message. All you can do is reread the letter, tell the world about it, and try to forget that someone you barely knew had loved you enough to die for you.'

'Maybe. But just imagine how pleased he'd be that you finally know about him. The two of you, from what I gathered in his journal, never really had a soulful, heart-to-heart talk.'

He nodded, and for the first time that morning, didn't affect to be pressed to head back to his office. He wanted to hear more. She too liked their impromptu coffee and wasn't against drawing it out.

'I wonder if having me know now,' he said, 'without being able to respond was not his way of making me wish he'd actually told me. I might have heard him out and at least laid out my reasons for saying no to him. It's as if by dying he robbed me of the right to hesitate, to argue back, or ask what he was really hoping to get from me.'

For the first time that morning, Carol let a tender smile lighten her features. Maybe Julian was far more generous than she had ever been with Paul. Maybe the boy, as she continued to think of him so as not to consider him a latter-day rival, might not have turned him down in the end. Or if he did, he'd have said it in a way that would have left Paul feeling grateful and pleased to have found the courage to speak.

'What isn't funny, from what I've been able to gather from his journal – and you are totally entitled to sit in the library and read the whole thing dating far back before your birth – is that he may not have wanted a relationship with either of us, which may be why he never confided his love to you. In my case, he was so resigned to accept failure that perhaps all he wanted was for me to know about it – as if it were a rumour, or just gossip whose origin wasn't established since he couldn't establish it in himself. We might, of course, be wrong in thinking he was too shy or too withdrawn to reveal his love. Maybe he didn't want to put you in an awkward position or embarrass you with his admission; he might have been keeping it under wraps, not for his sake, but for yours. Or maybe he knew you were already taken and didn't dare intrude. But here's the thing: had either of us said yes to him he would have turned that yes into a far-fetched

33

maybe. He was reluctant to trust what life had to offer, much less to act once the offer was on the table.'

Julian looked startled. 'I don't understand.'

'He held back from saying anything to you or to me over the years because he knew that what he was asking was not one night, or a week, or anything as binding as a life with us. What he was asking was something vague, like reluctant sympathy, or an understated nod that means to say *no* but says it evasively enough to sound like *Maybe later someday but not now*.

'By the time I knew him, he was altogether resigned not to hope for love in his life. He felt love, as he did on the night we shared together when he opened his heart to me and made love to me, but he either knew it was short-lived or that he wasn't really invited to the feast. If invited, it's because someone else had declined. Which is why he had the courage to tell me he loved me. Because he already knew

I'd turn him down, just as he knew he'd in all likelihood walk out of my life a few hours after spending a night with me. So yes, if it was love, it never stood a chance. As always with him, it was all in the head. What we've called his message in a bottle was nothing more than an attempt to make what never happened in his life turn into something that could have happened. And maybe this is what love is: finding someone who allows us to access not the life we've been given and were asked to live, but the life we're owed. This morning, Julian, we're each other's surrogates to Paul.

'Maybe by bringing us together he wanted you to realize that you liked him a bit more than you thought you did. Talking to you I now wish I'd told him so many, many things – that I loved his company, that I loved his very mind and the way he thought, that I even loved the books he recommended though I resisted reading them, because I didn't want to love blindly what he loved. Maybe what he wanted from the two of us, you and me, was for us to sit together for a while and grieve for him, which in his view is the closest thing to love.'

Julian took this in for a second.

'Nice job, Paul!' he cried. They exchanged smiles. Julian looked at her. She must be, what, mid-sixties? There was not a thing they had in common. How could Paul be in love with two persons who couldn't have been more different from each other?

Julian had long finished his coffee and was already playing with the cup. Carol had not touched hers. She stood up, then made a decisive gesture and poured the coffee onto a bush girding the area. 'Let's take a walk in the park. I don't like to leave things hanging.'

'Haven't they been hanging for close to fifty years?' he dared to ask.

She looked at him, smiled. *Bullseye*, she thought, but didn't say a word. She liked this man with the agile wit and the childish manner that probably screened his maturity.

'Was I totally off?' he ventured to ask, maybe by way of apologizing for the brusque remark.

'No.'

By the stairs leading to West 40th Street, she spotted a garbage receptacle and threw her empty cup into it. He swished his in, looked at her, almost expecting subdued applause for the college basketball player. None came. Of course, he thought. By now he'd figured her out: the type who always raises your bet but then reluctantly folds when you raise hers.

They tried to stay clear of the sun, though there was no way to avoid the blinding light bouncing off the sidewalk. 'I should have brought a hat and sunglasses,' she said. 'They said it will be boiling this weekend. Lucky you; you have the beach to look forward to.'

'We're having friends for dinner at the beach tonight. Light, cold stuff. My husband is the so-called chef. He's already at the beach. I mix the drinks. That's all I know to do. And God help anyone who asks for sangria. I hate sangria, not sure I even like people who like sangria.'

She let a moment pass. 'You must have strong feelings about sangria?'

He laughed. 'I wonder how my husband will react to the news when I tell him about Paul. He knew Paul too, through me and at receptions. The strange thing is that we never spoke about him. He never came up. I wonder now why we were so silent about him.'

'I think you're being too shrinkish.'

'Shrinkish does not exist in my Scrabble dictionary.'

She giggled, but let the comment pass. 'Would your husband be upset?'

'Would *your* husband be upset?' he retorted.

'My husband knew about it, but he never took it seriously. And besides, I married my husband, not Paul. To be perfectly honest, though, Paul would never have married me.

'He told me so himself. I asked him in passing once, years after we were both married, if he'd have wanted to marry me instead. I was so sure he wanted to but never had the courage to ask. I hadn't finished my question when, to my surprise, he right away blurted out an almost appalled "Never." "Why wouldn't you have?" I asked, seeing how blunt his answer was. Again, he gave himself no time to summon an elegant response: "Because you and I are identical. We'd tear each other apart. I read your mind, you read mine, I know every bend and tunnel in your scheming brain, and you know everything I've never had the guts to tell anyone. We are more intimate than husbands and wives – and yet we've barely slept together to pass for exes."

'I guess he was more dead-on than I thought – about not marrying me. I've spent two months reading him, feeling all along that he was skulking behind a wall, gauging my progress, nodding away with a *Gotcha, sister* each time he had me pegged. So, to answer your question, I'll never know why he never considered marrying me.'

'I could ask the same thing,' he said, 'why in five years he never once found the moment to let me know how he felt. Or to hint, or to let me infer. I wouldn't have laughed at him. Was he that closeted? I don't think so. All those large black-and-white photo portraits of naked Mauritanians lounging on the beaches on his office walls with glinting, come-hither glances and flaunting their huge schlongs at you because no one's ever seen anything like them in God's good kingdom – hard to imagine him prudish that way.'

She liked the image. She too had seen the

photos in his office. She told him that these photos had been taken by an Italian photographer called Luigi Bevilacqua.

'As far as I know, Luigi was the only man with whom he had a physical relationship. I met him once only and that was in passing. They were together for quite a while. Then his lover flew back to Italy. We never spoke about him. I wish we had. Whether Paul was in love with him or not, I'll never know. That's the thing about the dead. You know you've lost someone when you can't wait to ask them something and all you get when you're stupid enough to look for them is: *We're sorry, you have reached a number that has been disconnected or is no longer in service.* It's the most classic definition of death.'

'But doesn't talking about him disprove this?' he asked.

'I thought the case was closed and the ledger tossed into the fire,' she said, 'but here we are, prying it open and trying to rescue it from the embers. He wanted to stay billeted in our lives for however long he fancied. His shadow is still with us, call it his ghost.'

At this point, as they were loitering in the park toward Sixth Avenue, she finally said, 'Would you have another ten minutes for me? I like that we've talked about him. True, I have forty-plus years to work through. But I have absolutely no one to talk to, no one. Just you.'

He gave a compassionate nod. He'd known people his age who'd died and whose partners had no one left but him to talk to.

'But think how I must feel,' he said. 'I have to rewind the tape five years and question everything I remember, all those times we met, spoke, didn't speak, looked, or didn't. Who knows what I'll uncover. I'll think of the very few times we spoke – they all meld into a handful of scattered moments. I'm going to have to reinterpret what I can't remember.'

'Maybe you'll tell all your housemates tonight that you spent some time this morning with me discussing Paul.'

'They'll laugh me out of the room,' he said.

'Don't be silly. Can't you at least think of a moment in those five years when maybe . . . maybe you might have picked up a signal?'

He thought for a moment but didn't want to fall into what began to feel like a trap.

'From what I was able to gather from you, the signals would have been strewn just about everywhere. His invitations to his end-of-the-year shindigs in his office loft, his singling me out each time we ran into each other at Starbucks, his advice on where to travel, even where to stay, and then that day last year when he told me that he liked to do this one thing every Christmas.'

'What thing?'

'He bought me a bow tie. He arrives at our Starbucks, opens his duffel bag, produces this flat, rectangular orange box and apologizes for not wrapping it in gift paper. Yes, it was a signal, of course it was a signal, but did I register it as such? No.'

'Told your friends or your husband about the bow tie?'

He hesitated. This was the first time she noticed the young litigator baulk.

'Well, this will surprise you,' he said. 'I never told him – I told no one.'

She smiled with irony limned on her features.

'I don't need to interpret that silence, do I?'

He bit his lower lip. The young lawyer should know not to do this, she thought.

'How did you thank him?'

'I hugged him.'

'*You what? You* hugged *him!*'

She couldn't believe his words. That part was not in his journal.

'Wouldn't a prosecutor rest his case at this point?'

He looked at her with a mock-guilty, sly expression on his face.

'Yes, he would.'

'So, you didn't know or didn't want to know?'

That impish look crept back on his lips and eyes.

'Both, I think,' he said.

They crossed the street and ended on the shady side of 42nd Street.

'None of it matters. He died,' she said.

'Still, such a wasted life, don't you think?'

'Yes, but for the journal. If you ever read the journal, you'll find something quite singular. Throughout his entire life he lusted after so many people and was totally obsessed by them, sometimes for weeks on end, to say nothing of months or years. I blush at the things he says about so many he wished to sleep with. He didn't just have the hots for you, he wrote down the hots, what he wanted to do with you – graphic and explicit stuff. He was obsessive,'

45

she said, 'which is always easy to mistake for love. But he wasn't fooled. Obsession is not love. It looks like love, the way jealousy, anger, grief and even spite look like love. They are the distortions of love. Unless, of course, it's the other way around, which in typical, contrarian mode, he was also willing to accept, where obsession, jealousy and spite are the masks that love wears when it doesn't want to admit that someone has a strong pull on us. Was he in love when he knew he wasn't? Or was he already in love and didn't want to know it? Paul was fully aware of this paradox and was unforgiving with himself.'

She took out her phone and found the photo of the page in the journal, with the date affixed at the top of the page: *I'm not sure I've known love. I have never slept long enough with someone to know that I loved them. It's my fault. My life was filled with roundabout, makeshift loves, scattered about like craters and potholes,*

*all so vacant. Those that mattered never hap-
pened.'*

Julian was moved, in good part because up
till now, the journal was like the scroll of a
book that no longer exists except in poor tran-
scripts and in alleged copies of copies. But here
was a picture of the original. And the date at
the top of the picture said it all: seven months
ago, he thought. 'We might have been sitting
at Starbucks that morning, and he'd have been
his usual, wry, chipper self.'

'Same thought here,' she said. 'We'd have
dinner with him and his wife, sometimes
they'd bring along Anna Livia when she was
fourteen or so, and she'd always end up reading
or sulking in a corner. He'd be the one crack-
ing the jokes, telling us all manner of stories
about his travels and the famous painters,
authors and composers he knew. And yet, as
he's telling us the filthy joke about the hunter
who got lost in the forest, I'm sitting right in

front of him knowing that neither of us will ever talk of anything between us, while he, I suspect, was already drifting away from us.'

He was so focused on her that he didn't dare interrupt.

'And we're bursting out laughing,' she continued, 'including their daughter, who finally yields and joins in the laughter without knowing why we're all laughing, because her father knew how to tell a joke, and Paul, good man that he was, whom I probably will love to my dying day, suddenly stares at me when I'm not looking but knows I am looking just the same, even when my eyes are avoiding his, and asks, *Will there be a time to turn back the clock?*'

She smiled, and he smiled back, but this was no smiling matter, and they knew it.

'In our earliest days in college we used to go to the library, not just to translate George Orwell together and read Dante but also for the long walk afterwards. Then we'd head to a bar to order Irish coffees or black Russians, I can't remember which, just to be together.

'Our first kiss, of course, never comes up. We know that mentioning Irish coffees and the old bar – or our beloved movie theatre, which was cut up in four only to disappear eventually – any of these would have led us to the kiss, which hovered just steps away. He waited, and maybe I waited too, the two of us hoping the kiss might inadvertently crop up if only in a stirring glance, not realizing that we were no more than two individuals who've missed a bus they never really meant to take.

'The kisses that followed a year later when I did ask him upstairs after the party on Charles were feeble echoes of what we knew we were never going to relive together. But we grinned at the dinner table with our spouses because the slimmest scrap from our past still stirred something in us, or because the old air of mischief, which used to linger over everything

I'd start saying and that he'd invariably finish for me, had not perished. It was still alive and may be the one thing I, or he, or the two of us still missed without ever claiming we did. We laughed it off together, but the joke was on us. While he was being ever so merry with the world, he was already packing it in, waving farewell with a broad smile. So, we should never say *only yesterday he was in the best of moods, or in the best health.* Paul was already headed to what he called the *Big Blank.* There was nothing to live for, done with planet earth, done with life.

'All this perhaps is my way of saying to you that for a man as withdrawn and so self-effacing as he was, have you any idea what it meant for him to buy you a necktie? Do you know that if he didn't wrap it, it's because he wanted to lessen its impact. A great gift offered like an afterthought, a mere bauble, *Give it to someone else if you don't like it.* I can just hear Paul saying, *Oh, and I got you this.*'

'That's exactly how he said it,' interjected Julian. 'What an operator. And yet he's the one not sure he's known love. Not exactly the best send-off for my weekend at the beach. But still.' He paused a moment. 'We've all had bad lovers, we've all been with people we'd give fortunes never to have met. But never to have shared a bed long enough with someone you might have loved . . . I'd take my own life if I got to be his age and never held someone I loved naked in my arms,' he added with a smile. 'It would be like dying a virgin. Or having lived for nothing.'

Only after saying this did he realize that this was precisely what Paul had done: lived for nothing then taken his own life.

'Then why didn't you pick up the hint when he gave you that tie? He described the hug: he touched your face with both his hands, and you put your hand on the back of his neck.'

'He did not!'

'It's in his journal! Paul noticed everything. There are things about me, descriptions of clothes I wore just a few times, things I had completely forgotten but that he had noted down. He was scrupulous to a fault. The way I looked at him sometimes, the way you looked at him – nothing escaped him. If he says he touched your face with both hands, then he touched your face with both hands. You just failed to notice.'

'Did I throw him under the bus?'

'No, you didn't,' she said with a listless and forgiving tone. 'And he never held a thing against you. But I did – throw him under the bus, that is – and the sad part is that I must have done it many times over, and most times without even realizing it.'

They walked back toward the Grill and could tell from across the street that the place had reopened. Carol said she would not say no to chilled mineral water, but that she remembered he had those phone calls to make and all these things to do before heading to the beach. His answer surprised her. 'The phone calls can wait. Actually,' he said with that grin on his features that betrayed his shyness, 'I may have exaggerated.'

'In case I was a dreadful bore.'

'Yes,' he confessed.

They crossed the street and entered the Bryant Park Grill and ordered a large bottle of San Pellegrino. She wanted a cup of coffee.

'Why, because you never drank the earlier one?' he asked.

She looked at him with a playful smile.

'You just sounded like him. This is exactly what he would have said, reminding you that he had noticed you hadn't drunk the first coffee. He would have logged that insignificant fact in his mind, saved it for later without even knowing he was saving it, and then when the moment came, he'd spring it on you, and you'd both laugh. I guess that after five years you picked up a few things.'

He took what sounded like a compliment without saying a word.

'And by the way, that coffee – dreadful.'

'But Paul used to like it, I still do.'

She ordered two cups of coffee.

'Hot or cold?' asked the waiter.

'Hot, of course,' she snapped, 'unless—' she said, turning to Julian.

'Hot for me too.'

'I hate ice in my mouth.'

'And I hate sangria.'

It made the two of them laugh again – another signature moment that reminded her of Paul. He liked to repeat things that became funny by virtue of being repeated. She looked at him. She liked him. She could see why Paul liked him too.

As they were waiting: 'I have no idea if they'll make the journal public one day, but I am so glad I read it through. You have permission to read it too, I could send you a copy of it. You may never want to look at his pages or know more than what I've told you, but at least you've spoken with me and know that something exists out there with your name on it. So, as far as I'm concerned, mission accomplished.'

'I don't know. Everything you've opened up leaves an unfinished taste. Like finding that you're seriously in debt but know you've never borrowed anything from anyone. Still, the dunning notice lands at your door. And the strange thing is that you can't even pay it because the creditor is dead and has left no heirs. You must pay, but how, to whom?'

'Death does that,' said Carol.

'The funny thing is that I should have asked him very plainly about his gift, made him tell me something.'

'But don't you see? He wouldn't have told you anything and his answer would have been a non-answer, a disclaimer, *give it to someone else if you don't like it.'*

Julian looked totally dumbfounded.

'Do you wish he'd told you, or even broached the subject?' she asked.

The question stumped him once again.

'I don't know. Maybe not.'

'So, silence was his only option?'

'Maybe.'

A cordial, understanding look passed between them as if to mean, *What more is there to say?* She shrugged her shoulders with distracted restraint then folded her napkin and placed it back on the table.

'Would you have been his lover if you'd known that a simple *yes* might have prevented his death?' he asked.

'Yes.' Hers was a decisive answer. 'But I would have regretted it, as I'm sure he would too, maybe more than I. And we knew this not just after, but even before making love the first time. Ours was a one-night stand, but never more. I recovered, but it destroyed him. It annihilated entire years of his life, which is why we kept each other at bay. We didn't want to know what we might have missed, nor did we want to know what might have turned into one big nothing. How about you? Would you have said yes to stop him from killing himself?'

'Funny you should ask. Probably, or just maybe. I don't quite think that I liked him that way. I might have slept with the man who would have died, not with the living man himself. I did grow to like him, though. Perhaps I'd end up liking him that way too if I were single and didn't have Dennis in my life, but we'll never know.'

She added a thought. 'What killed it in us both was silence and shame. Silence and shame had stopped him with you too. Shame is what we feel when we want something from someone, shame holds our tongue, and then

57

silence sits on it and never lets up.'

There was nothing to add or to say after this. Maybe a few blandishments about the weather, their personal lives, her children, the house he shared with friends on the beach, her forthcoming trip to Sicily, oh, and let's not forget the volleyball match, she added with a mirthful, convivial smile.

Their coffee finally arrived. Would they be ordering lunch, asked the waiter. 'No, just coffee if you don't mind,' she replied. There it was again, that snarky tone that didn't quite match the genuine affability she'd shown over the past half hour. She had started caustic, was guileless, even mellow with Julian, but in a second could turn caustic all over again. She'd just done it with the waiter. Even her thank you when he poured the San Pellegrino seemed graceless and snippy. She stared at the neat, polished wedges of lime in their glasses.

'Do you like him?' she asked.

'Who?'

'The waiter, whom else?'

'He's handsome.'

'Very handsome,' she said, 'clearly an actor, though more in your camp, I think.' There was a lambent, almost taunting tone in her voice, as if she were trying to have him admit he was attracted or maybe coax him into charming the young man. After the waiter turned away, Julian gave him a long, second look, but he knew he was doing it more to please her.

'Was Paul in your camp, you think?' she asked. But then sensing she'd either overstepped or used a word so obsolete as to sound borrowed from a prudish, different age, she added, 'I was just asking, my friend.' She was trying to apologize, hoping the brusque tone of her question hadn't caused the taken-aback look on his face.

But he noticed her change of tone. The woman was not only soft-spoken when she wanted to be, but behind her sharp, snappy manner she could be unusually sweet, even diffident and self-effacing. Gone the acerbic tone simply because he had looked her straight in the face and had seemingly questioned her use of the word 'camp' when she could easily have used another word or even not broached the subject at all. He could almost see how beneath her abrupt manner she shared Paul's ability to read others and to slant her tone to theirs so that not a ripple would stand between them. This was Paul's manner of dodging sensitive spots and above all of extending an olive branch if he offended someone unintentionally. Sometimes the olive preceded the offence, which told the young litigator that Paul always knew where his sentences were headed long before he'd even uttered them.

'To be perfectly honest – and this will tell you how shallow I am – I never thought he was interested in me, let alone in men,' said

Julian. 'I might have given him a hug once, but that was as impetuous as I got with him.'

'Yes, and he noticed, and knew better than to make more of it than it was. He wrote that he let go of you before you did. So typical. He'd been longing to touch you and yet when you hugged him, he let go first.

'The last time I kissed him we were still young,' she said. 'We had been to a party and were already looking back at our years as platonic friends. However, I was eager for passion that night, or maybe I was finally feeling something for him. We kissed at the doorway to my building. This time, though, what I got was the most feckless, faint-hearted kiss a man ever gave a woman. He wanted me desperately, I could tell, but he held back. As with your hug, he was the one who ended the kiss, not I. With anyone else I would have chalked it up to a mistake; but with him it was no mistake. He was holding back because he had learnt not to trust that this was real, that it could have led somewhere but that it wasn't going to.

'In the end, not trusting became his default setting, with me, with you, with everyone. We went upstairs, slept together, had breakfast, made love again. The next morning we said goodbye. I didn't see him again for several years. This suited me fine. And him too, I suspect. Normally, what we seek in someone is not our opposite but our mirror self, because someone who is us defies all boundaries, including those of time. It's happening to me right now. As I told you earlier, he is not dead to me; he is still around, though not altogether present. But I dream of him. And sometimes I still speak to him, as he's often confessed in his journal that he liked speaking aloud to me when I wasn't there and no one could hear. As for you, it's much simpler: you offered him the portrait of the life he should have had in his younger days and of the person he should have been and would have loved to be. Nothing I know speaks love more eloquently. I'm not jealous; I'm envious.'

'When I happened to read of his death in the paper,' he said, 'I was saddened. I even caught myself still hoping to run into him at our usual Starbucks to ask him if that story I'd read about him in the paper was actually true. I missed him. Since reading the obit, I tried not to go there, though I still go back because it's close to the office. Little did I know until this morning that he used to go there for me, just for me. It forces me to re-evaluate everything, how I read people, what effect I have on them, who I am and whom others see when they cross paths with me. I am more persuaded than ever now that I am someone I never knew I was. When I go to get my cup of coffee on Tuesday morning, I'll miss him much more this time, especially after today. All that work, all that effort, and the anxiety, and the waiting, and the hoping – to say nothing of the debilitating awkwardness. But he came every morning, just the same, and all for me. Think of the damage I caused—'

'No, I did that,' she broke in. 'By the time he fell for you he was already a damaged soul. He knew he was damaged. And for that he had no one to blame but me. I forced him to trade an unlived life for a life misspent. I killed something in him. Passion? Trust? Vigour? Fun? Who'll ever know. After me, he shut down, like those mom-and-pop pharmacies that struggle to stay open by brandishing bottles of vitamins, reading glasses and sundry household goods like colanders and salad-spinners. He was as good as dead already but plodded on. He lost who he was, as if someone had put a lien on him and owned him and spoke over him when all he wanted was to hear his old voice again. Someone robbed his soul, and that someone was me. Maybe he wanted to find it

again with you. But he was living in hock and
the loan was never forgiven. Perhaps he and
I should have lived together even if we'd split
soon after. Perhaps I was the one scared, not
he. Perhaps so many things.'

She gave what she'd just said further con-
sideration. Then she raised her shoulders as
though dismissing a stray thought.

'You know, on very rare occasions, he and
I spoke about the friendship that had bound
us so many years earlier, but almost always as
though the persons we'd been once were far-
away dead relatives whom we still liked to
make fun of. But you, when you came on the
scene, were his last hope. I was his first, you his
last. Whoever came in between didn't matter.'

'You think so?'

'I think so. Something happens to someone
whose life has run its course. He hides it, as
he hid with me and then with you, and from
himself too. The Starbucks thing, the person

65

without a pronoun, the jokes at our dinner table – what a performance. He was like the guy who gets back home after a wonderful dinner party and the moment he turns on the light in his living room decides either to walk out the front door again or to take his own life. Paul was so, so bored.'

'I still can't understand why he did it,' said Julian. 'Wasn't there a sign? Right now, I'm trying to rewind to the beginnings of our tenuous friendship, but I can't remember a thing. I know we kept crossing paths when buying coffee in the morning, but how long that lasted, I have no idea. This, I am sure, is the part that must have galled him: that I had no idea of anything. It went on for five years, you say? Was he never going to say a word?'

'Paul was that way.'

'But doesn't someone break down, doesn't our tongue trip, or hopes to slip if the will or courage to speak can't be roused?'

'Silence and shame, Julian.'

'This could easily have gone on for another ten years: Starbucks in the morning with me, and dinners with your spouses. As I turn back the clock, it's clear to me that I wasn't interested or attracted – he was just some older guy who says hello but who never buttonholes you. Even after we'd become sort-of-acquaintances and spoke more liberally, he was frequently the one who left Starbucks first. I noticed this because though he was usually there before me, he would eventually look at his watch and say, "Time to migrate" – those were his actual words. But who could have guessed the rest? That he sat there waiting for me and no one else? That he would leave to avoid looking like a hanger-on?

'Then one day – could have been last year, or the year before – there he is, seated at his usual spot with his usual pencil, editing what looked like a typewritten manuscript. By then we always greeted each other and no longer uttered token hellos. Instead, he waved a mirthful, buoyant salutation from across the store and said, "I need your opinion." "My opinion as a lawyer?" I asked, already nervous that here was another person eager to hock me for free legal advice. "Not legal opinion. I have lawyers for that," he said. "I just need to sort something out and I can't decide." I asked if I could leave my briefcase with him while I ordered coffee and something to eat.

'When I sat down with my breakfast, it turned out that he had been invited to China and didn't want to visit any place but Shang-hai. But then the conversation turns out to be about his reason for going to China, a place he'd always managed to avoid. Was it good for business? I asked. "Yes, it would open many doors and bring in a lot of new money." So, he'd have to go, I concluded. Yes, he knew that. Still, he asked, why was he so indifferent to a country that many people would give their right hand to visit? "It's either that I freeze before the unknown and try to avoid what I don't know or that I'm scared I'll hate China and wouldn't be able to leave until a week later." "This is more about you than about China," I remember saying. "I may not like new things," he said, "or there is a countervailing impulse in me that really longs for new things. Maybe what truly scares me is that I'll end up loving China. Then what?" I liked the way he was opening up to me. I liked his friendship. If there was a subtext to what he was saying, I was deaf to it.

'Eventually we ended up leaving Starbucks with our coffees in hand and walking, just as you and I did this morning. Then, after reaching Sixth Avenue we turned around and came back and headed to Starbucks to purchase another cup of coffee each. He paid using the app on his iPhone. He liked showing that he knew how to use the app. I'm sure it made him feel young. Eventually, he walked me all the way to my building. We shook hands. We ended up discussing his trip to China many more mornings afterward. He never went to China. But it's that one long walk devoted to China that I'll always remember.'

She sensed that what Paul said about China was little more than his way of confiding something about himself, maybe even about his sexuality.

Then, suddenly, she saw it. 'I know what he was doing. I just know what my good old, cunning little Paul was doing.'

'What?'

'All that talk about China. He wanted you to say you'd been dying to visit China. At which point he would have turned around and said he'd go if you went with him.' She gave a little chuckle. 'But you said no such thing.'

'I did not.'

'It was a desperate try. Or maybe it was his way of telling himself that he had at least tried and, knowing him, he was probably grateful you'd failed to pick up the cue. He was terrified he'd love your company, the way he was terrified he'd love China. Unless . . .'

'Unless?'

'Unless the whole China thing was all made up and he was just looking for an excuse to spend time chatting with you and opening up to you.'

Julian had nothing to say. Carol didn't either. During the silence, she dug into her large leather bag and took out a thick manila envelope. She opened it and produced a slim, leather-bound volume.

'My husband had a hundred copies printed on very nice paper then added a calfskin cover so people could keep it somewhere visible instead of stowing it away.'

'Are these excerpts from Paul's journal?'

'Oh, no. It's a fairy tale he wrote about two years ago.'

'But this must have cost a fortune. Even I can tell it's calfskin,' he said.

'Yes, it is. We're planning to send one to each of our friends. You are the first to receive a copy.'

He held the slim volume and felt its smooth cognac leather binding. He smelled it, then brought the volume against his cheek. 'It feels wonderful,' he said.

'We wanted the best leather, so this one is from Italy. But it comes with one condition.'

'What condition?'

'Spoken like a lawyer,' she said. 'It's my condition, not his, of course. I think he would have wanted you to read it once a year, maybe on July 2nd, his birthday – today, that is. It's less than three thousand words long, so it might take you, what, ten minutes?'

Julian opened the cryptic little work and

read its title: *The Rose and the Artichoke*. 'What is it about?' he asked.

'It's a story about a rose who falls in love with an artichoke. The rose kept an eye on the artichoke from the day she spotted him, and he in turn watched her grow, from bud to stem to the most resplendent blossom, a sterling pink he caught sight of each morning. Their love, for love it was, when she stared and he stared back, horrified every plant, flower, vegetable and insect in the kingdom.

'One night, ignoring everyone's vigilance and going against the decree that no rose should ever turn to love a stodgy, ageing, fat and leafy artichoke, the rose let her stem grow so long that she was finally able to slip away from the rosebush to reach the artichoke and twirl herself around his stem seven times to draw close to his big heart. The chameleon, who had cleared the way for her passage, told her that she had shortened her days and

73

hours by travelling so far to reach him. But she doesn't care. They spend the night embraced together, but in the morning—'

'He wrote it?'

'Yes, Paul wrote it.'

'But why are my three initials on the leather cover?'

'Because' – and she looked straight at him, almost shaking her head to mean *Shouldn't it be obvious by now?* – 'because it's about you.'

Julian looked totally stumped.

'How do you know?' he asked.

'Because it's in his journal, for Christ's sake. It was his last attempt to fantasize, and he knew it was fantasy: he, the old artichoke, you, the young rose, all of it wishful thinking. He was asking for the moon. Don't you see?'

'But he never even asked.'

'Who really asks for the moon?'

Julian promised to read it that very afternoon on the way to the beach. He'd be riding the train by himself, as everyone would already be lounging in the sun by then.

Once again, he brought the booklet very close to his face, undecided whether he wanted to smell it or rub his lips against its smooth skin. '*The Rose and the Artichoke*,' he mused. 'What a sad fate. What a very sad fate, our Paul.'

'Yes.' She thought for a moment, then added, 'Sadder yet, because it involves us and reminds us that his life was in our hands, though he no longer brought up his past with me – and as for you, how could you know anything when he kept so tight a lid on it. But can we pretend not to be aware of how he felt, knowing what we know now?'

'I don't know,' said Julian. 'I'd like to think that a very tiny part of me might even have allowed the thought to cross my mind. Had I ever made a pass at him, he would very politely have told me I was barking up the wrong tree. Paul was ambivalent with you because he was also drawn to men, but if he was ambivalent with me, it's because he was always drawn to you. He was after some kind of proof about himself, but for him seeking proof was as scary as the proof itself.'

'Maybe what he wanted from us was proof, not love. Which may also explain why he was so tentative about so many things. Everything had to be ascertained.'

'No,' said Julian. 'If he wanted proof, it's because love was already there, but he minced it into a scatter of tiny, querulous pieces voided of all life. I think he was in love, but his mind and his heart were never aligned. Something was always off, as if you and I were two stops on an endless train ride whose last station, as far as he knew, hadn't been built yet.'

'We'll never know.'

'Sometimes I look at men of his generation and all I want to do is scream and say, *How couldn't you have known by the time you were nine or ten?* Men of his generation did not know that they liked or even preferred men; for them this attraction was incidental, episodic, a minor distraction in their sexual lives that would peter away once they learnt to ignore it. A good night's sleep and the whole thing turned to vapour. But it always came back. Some didn't realize how strong the drive was. Many didn't even want to say its name, because it had too many syllables. But it had a name, and they wouldn't pronounce it, didn't even like the sound of the word or what it stood for, especially if applied to them. In short, it was routinely disowned, ignored, withheld and never taken seriously.

'Some like Paul had no way to reside in this strange world where they weren't convinced they belonged; they could enter it but only as foreigners who couldn't speak the language and whose true home, they thought, lay thousands of leagues away, while the very

77

shore on which they stood looking out to sea was their one and only home. They had fantasies, I was a fantasy.

'I don't have to read his journals, but I bet his pages teem with broken fantasies. If I am right,' continued Julian, 'everything he touched felt wrong, was wrong. In the end, all he did was think of what he never had till he was left with nothing. As you said, earth was wrong, and life was wrong. His whole life needed to be done over, and for that he needed time, and time had run out. Paul, the man who may never have been himself, the man who lived the wrong life and who can't buy himself back; Paul was the shadow of someone who never was, a stowaway in his own ship. He lived the wrong life, with you and with me and everyone he slept with, male and female. The rose never reached the artichoke, the rose never left the flower bed, the rose died alone. Paul wasn't just the artichoke, he was the rose too, you see. Or he was neither. He was like the chameleon, constantly shuttling and running errands between the two, forever changing colours because he had none.'

Carol listened, her eyes incredulous. 'I used to think that if he never pushed things with me, it's because he was scared and feared he'd never measure up to the sort of man he thought I wanted.'

'This might be your vanity speaking, Carol. If he was scared – and I'm not saying he wasn't – it wasn't because he thought he'd never be who you wanted. What he feared was disappointment. Not yours, but his. Where would he be, who would he be if we were wrong for him?'

The young man might have figured Paul to perfection, she thought. And without really knowing him.

'How do you know so much about what someone like Paul felt?'

79

'I used to know a man who would look at young male couples and admire them and wonder how simple and natural it was for them to find and share what their hearts and bodies wanted.'

'A man? Who was he?'

Julian paused a moment.

'He was my father. When I brought Dennis to my parents' home, for the first time, my father couldn't believe that here were two young men who not only accepted who they were together, but who thrived and had found love without struggle and with nothing to fear or hide. It was our ease and complete normalcy that disarmed him.'

'What did your father do?'

'What did he do? The very next day he called me at the office to say he envied me. His words. As we'd dropped in on them unannounced the previous evening, he'd watched how carefully Dennis had laid down the silverware on my side of the table and then folded the cloth napkin for me. In his elderly view, what happened between men was nothing short of dirty, vicious, bathroom stuff – not love. Then he said it was too late for him. I told him there was no such thing as too late. "There are no chapters left in my book," he said. "Then write the next," I said, thinking I was giving solid advice.'

'Did he do anything?'

'He never told me, I never asked. I've never forgiven myself for that smug metaphor. But I've often wondered why I never asked. Probably, I feared what he might do or what would happen to my mother. Or what's more likely, I didn't want to think that my father's marriage was a sham, or, worse yet, that I was the child of a sham. But then, aren't we all children of one sham or another?'

Suddenly, something alighted on Julian's features. As if in digging into himself he had discovered a deeper, unexpected layer.

'I'm having second thoughts, Carol. What if I were just a cover for Paul, a distraction, a sort of necessary alibi to prevent him from seeing that the only love he'd ever nursed in life was you and that after a few years it was time to realize you were forever lost to him? Maybe I, and most likely other men before me, were just decoys.'

'Interesting,' she replied. 'By the same token, though, maybe I myself was a decoy and you his real love.'

They both laughed. 'We'll never solve this cat's cradle.'

'Neither could Paul,' she said. 'Which might explain why his journals number thousands of pages. He was trying to figure something out that self-knowledge couldn't uncover. Typical, typical, Paul. Was he in love with us, or was he in lust, or was he just compulsive because compulsion was the closest thing to his heart?'

'Come to think of it,' added Julian, 'maybe there was neither a rose nor an artichoke in his life. One never beckoned, the other never budged. This applies to almost all people who stand and wait.'

'True.' She looked him square in the face. She had grown to like him. 'I'm beginning to see now why he sought you out every morning.'

'I was going to say the same about you.'

'Why?' she asked.

'Because behind the curtishness in your overall manner, you're an unusually sweet, deep and understanding person.'

'Curtish isn't a Scrabble word.'

'Rhymes with shrinkish and soonish.'

'I never said shrinkish or soonish.'

'Yes, you did.'

'Did I really?'

'May I hug you?' he asked.

She nodded. *Of course.*

As they were hugging: 'You're hugging him, aren't you?' he said.

'No different than you are.'

83

'Different is not an adverb,' said the young lawyer.

Both chuckled and gave each other a second hug before separating.

'Promise to read it on the train? It's like his Christmas present to the two of us.'

'Promise.'

'One last question.' She hesitated. 'Do you think Paul might have had something else in mind in asking us to meet?'

He gave a very vague shrug. *Who's to know?*

Carol looked at him with a puckish flicker in her eyes. 'I don't think so either. But Paul's mind was twisted and ran through endless mazes with all manner of recoils and double doors. I still think he might have wanted us to draw closer to each other, to become good friends, lifelong, intimate friends, and through us, earn what life never gave him.

'Or maybe all he wanted was for us to love him and by talking about him allow his spirit to hover a while longer in our lives. Not much to ask, don't you think? He did not fear the *Big Blank*, but he didn't want people to forget him; maybe he wanted them to grieve for him. But the last thing he wanted was to leave a distorted or befouled face behind, so that people would want to look away. Not for him the window or the high bridge, nothing messy.'

There was a moment of silence.

'So, you're off to the beach?'

'No, first to the office and then to Penn Station.'

Then she asked him, 'Can I call you in about a month's time – just to chat maybe?'

'Funny, I was going to ask you the same thing,' he said.

'He'd have loved that.'

'I know,' said Julian.

He stood up and left the Grill, which is when, on watching him walk away and close the heavy glass door behind him, Carol thought that he might never leaf through the journal, maybe not even glance at the leather-bound gift, which he'd most likely leave in his office. And this, once again, left her feeling totally lonely, as if a cruel injustice had been committed and she was mourning Paul all over again, except that this time she was doing it alone, and would always mourn him alone. At best, Julian might write a short email thanking her and never write again. Or maybe she was wrong about Julian. We'll see, she thought.

She had meant to ask him if he thought she too was a stowaway in her own life. Were Julian and Dennis stowaways too? She didn't think so. At least not yet. One becomes a stow-away when there's nothing left to look forward to and all one does then is look back and question everything.

As Carol left the Grill and began walking toward Grand Central to take the subway home, it finally dawned on her that Paul was

really gone. They would never run into each
other again, never talk, or ever remind each
other of so many details that either one of them
might have forgotten. In the months since he
died as she kept reading his journal, he seemed
almost close at hand, and, provided she didn't
look back to catch him looking over her shoulders as she turned page after page, she could
almost feel his breath. Perhaps he wasn't quite
gone, just hovering somewhere but never far. In
her own way, she'd done what those who miss
the dead do when they hold on to their sweat-
ers, pillowcases and outworn, ragged winter
coats, which they refuse to send to the cleaner's,
hoping their smell will linger on until someone
either gives them away or has them laundered,
and then the smell is gone forever and all that
stays behind are photographs, some videos
and their voice on their answering machine.
Carol had taped his just in time before his wife
removed it – then he'd be good and gone, and

there'd be no one, not one soul left with whom she could discuss his death or remember their years together. She had thought that Julian might be a bridge to him, but he was scarcely a wooden plank, mindlessly thrown over a puddle on a rainy day and then as hastily removed when the rain stopped. Suddenly she saw that the only person who would have understood and allowed her to unload the swell of grief that seized her late that morning as she headed to the Lexington Avenue train would have been none other than the dead man himself, and he was gone for good.

So, you're dead, she thinks.

Good and buried, he replies.

Why did you do it?

Why? Simple. I was so bored I had been dead for so very long, don't you see?

That's not a reason. Is where you are any better now?

Much. I'm trying to forget you.

88

I haven't forgotten.

You will.

I miss you more than ever these days.

He doesn't reply.

How is it down there? she asks.

Why, want to come for a visit? he asks.

Gallows humour, but she laughs all the same.

I thought it would be better than living. But it really isn't.

I could have told you that.

And besides, my foot itches and I'm so trapped in this damned box they put me in that I can't even reach for my toe, let alone a passing handshake to Sir Lochinvar down beyonder with his slatternly two sisters.

How we laughed about down beyonder in the season of our sweet sighs, do you remember?

How couldn't I? I still think of you.

She remembers their Dante of so many years before.

Deh, he whispers,

Quando tu sarai tornato al mondo

E riposato de la lunga via . . .

Ricorditi di me, che son la Pia:

Siena mi fé, disfecemi Maremma:

Salsi colui che 'nnanellata pria

Disposando m'avea con la sua gemma.

Silence.

Then silence again.

You're not speaking to me, she says.

Silence.

I can't keep feeding you the words.

Silence again. And forever now.

The *Big Blank* was his name for it.

She is alone. This is what death means: you speak and no one answers. All she remembers is how they used to laugh together.

She remembers the summer weekday when he'd called her at the office, and they had lunched together in some sidewalk bistro in SoHo called The Albatross. Maybe the happiest day in her life, the happiest in his too. 'What would you do if I died,' he'd asked after telling her that a week earlier he was persuaded he'd be dying of bone cancer. He wanted to hear her say she'd be very sad. *I'd go to the theatre with my husband or to Federico's with friends and drink to your health.* He hadn't expected that answer, and it showed on his face. 'Idiot,' she'd blurted out. 'You'd erase my whole life if you died.'

When she reaches the train station and is standing on the platform, waiting for the uptown local, which takes forever to arrive, she pulls out her phone and for the nth time in her life rereads what he'd written about his death.

Death is a long, long void, far larger than the sum total of all the constellations in the universe lying trillions of light years away, where even God isn't waiting at the end of the road, because there is no end to that road. Death is everlasting and, even after the universe is swallowed up and rolled up into a tiny speck, death will outlast that speck.

She had wanted to read this to Julian. But one thing led to another and she forgot.

As she waits for the subway to arrive, she knows that something in her has died as well. It died nearly half a century before but she's always refused to know it. And maybe this was Paul's lesson: one dies a piece at a time, till there's no time, and no one to show us the exit – we die alone. He died alone.

She feels the surge of a wave so powerful that it has to be pity. And then it occurs to her that pity is the surest sign of love. Paul would have said that, because that too was the kind of thing he'd say. It brings a smile to her face. We become those we love. That was also Paul. He had never said it but, once again, the thought bore his imprint. *Oh, Paul,* she thinks, *did you have to die?*

She remembers the reception following his burial, with Connie focused on the guests while two servers keep offering all manner of exotic finger foods. Carol sneaks into his study, and there they are: his eyeglasses neatly folded where he left them on his desk, still waiting for him to come back and wear them, the shoe trees he was so fond of, the ashtrays he stopped using but still liked to see scattered around the house, the mementos that he treasured without being attached to them, the pictures of when he was a boy, the mug he liked because she had given it to him – all left behind for those who'll never know what to do with them and will keep them for decades until those who come after will throw them away to remind us that despite our best efforts, we'll be, yes, forgotten.

The train arrives, the doors open, she gets in, finds a seat, and no sooner is she in the car than she takes out her Kindle and opens it to Turgenev. 'A bright spring day was fading into evening.' Paul had asked her to read the novel long ago and, now that he's gone, she finally allows herself to love what he loved. She can almost hear his voice reading the words now, touching her ear with his lips. She is not alone, she thinks, yet she is more alone than ever now. 'A bright spring day was fading into evening.' He'll understand. But did they really know or understand what kept them bound? It isn't friendship, and it isn't love, though it could only be both love and friendship. But she doesn't know, and neither did he.

Then, lifting her head from her book, she thinks of *The Rose and the Artichoke*. She trusts Julian will read it. She wants to trust, and in trusting, hopes the dead man finds a semblance of rest now. She thinks of Julian on the crowded train to the Hamptons, and she thinks of his reading parts of the tale to everyone at dinner that night, or maybe just to Dennis later that same night when he'll tell him about his morning chat outside the Grill – yes, for five long years, who'd have guessed, a stowaway in his own ship, poor guy. Dennis looks at him and asks whoever is the artichoke who hasn't longed for a rose, at which Julian asks who is the rose who hasn't dared span the distance? Some rush to speak their heart, others stand and wait. I didn't wait, says Dennis. I didn't either, says Julian. We're lucky. Well, we are lucky, very lucky. Not stowaways, then? Never stowaways.

Enigma Variations

From the global bestselling author of Call Me by Your Name *and* Find Me

From a youthful infatuation with a cabinet maker in a small Italian fishing village to a passionate yet sporadic affair with a woman in New York, to an obsession with a man he meets at a tennis court, *Enigma Variations* charts one man's path through the great loves of his life. Paul's intense desires, losses and longings draw him closer, not to a defined orientation, but to an understanding that 'heartache, like love, like low-grade fevers, like the longing to reach out and touch a hand across the table, is easy enough to live down'.

André Aciman casts a shimmering light over each facet of desire, to probe how we ache, want and waver, and ultimately how we sometimes falter and let go of the very ones we want the most. We may not know what we want. We may remain enigmas to ourselves and to others. But sooner or later we discover who we've always known we were.

'Magnificent.' *New York Times*
'Unforgettable.' *Times Literary Supplement*
'Exquisite.' *New Yorker*

Available in paperback and ebook and audio.

faber

Out of Egypt

A transporting memoir from the global bestselling author

Aciman's story of Alexandria is the story of his own family: a Jewish family with Italian and Turkish roots that tied its future to Egypt and made its home there for three generations, only to find itself peremptorily expelled by the government in the early 1960s. It is the story of a fractious clan of dreamers and con men and the emotional price they would pay for exile, the story of a young boy's coming of age and his memories of the city he loved in his youth.

'[A] mesmerizing portrait of a now vanished world.' *New York Times*
'A dazzling evocation of a time and a place.' *Telegraph*
'Aciman . . . recalls with a magical sensibility streaked with antic humour.' *Publishers Weekly*

Available in paperback and ebook and audio.

faber

Also by André Aciman

The Gentleman from Peru

From the global bestselling author of Call Me by Your Name *and* Find Me

We spend more time than we know trying to go back. We call it fantasizing, we call it dreaming . . . but we're all crawling back, each in his or her own way.

A group of college friends find themselves marooned at a luxurious hotel on the Amalfi Coast in Italy. While their boat is being repaired, they can't help but observe the daily routine of a fellow hotel guest – a mysterious, white-bearded stranger who sits on the veranda each night and smokes one cigarette, sometimes two. When the group decide to invite the elegant traveller to lunch with them, they cannot begin to imagine his miraculous abilities, strange wisdom, and the life-changing story he is about to impart to one of the friends in particular . . .

Deeply atmospheric and sensual, *The Gentleman from Peru* weaves achingly poignant insight into a story of regret, fate and epic love.

'Another masterful tale of longing and desire.' *Glamour*
'You don't so much read André Aciman's novels as tumble breathlessly into them.' *The Times*

Available in paperback and ebook.

faber

Also by André Aciman

My Roman Year

The new memoir from the global bestselling author

1960s Rome. As teenage André stands on the dock, his mother fusses over their luggage – thirty-two suitcases, trunks and tea chests that contain their world. The ship will refuel and return to Alexandria, the home where they have left their father, as the Aciman family begin a new adventure in Rome. André is now head of the family, with a little brother to keep in line and a mother to translate for – for although she's mute, she is nothing if not communicative.

Equal parts transporting and beautiful, this coming-of-age memoir shares the luminous, fragile truth of life for a family forever in exile, living in Rome, but still yet to find a home.

'Transporting . . . sensuous.' *Observer*
'Compelling and witty.' *New Statesman*
'Aciman pieces together a rich tapestry of human emotion in a way few other contemporary writers can match.' *Dazed*

Available in paperback and ebook and audio.

faber

Also by André Aciman

Room on the Sea

From the global bestselling author of Call Me by Your Name *and* Find Me

Have you ever had the sense that maybe all lives are nothing more than the chronicle of countless stinging might-have-beens that continue to haunt us?

In the scorching New York heat, a hundred people wait to be selected as jurors. Paul is reading a newspaper. Catherine is reading a novel. So begins a whirlwind flirtation: over cappuccinos in Manhattan and gallery trips to Chelsea, Paul and Catherine escape into the illusion of an Italian getaway. Their feelings quickly evolve into something deeper, something – as mature adults with lives of their own – Paul and Catherine must carry on in secret, with the understanding that anything more than a casual crush is out of the question.

But as the sultry summer week draws to a close, the end of their rendezvous comes into focus, and Paul and Catherine are forced to decide whether to act on their feelings or leave the fantasy of what could have been to the annals of the past.

'A top-notch beach read.' *Daily Mail*
'Absorbing.' *Mail on Sunday*
'The perfect escapist read.' *i* newspaper

Available in paperback and ebook.

faber